Bibliographic information published by the German National Library:

The German National Library lists this publication in the National Bibliography; detailed bibliographic data are available on the Internet at http://dnb.dnb.de .

Imprint:

Copyright © 2016 GRIN Verlag, Open Publishing GmbH
Print and binding: Books on Demand GmbH, Norderstedt Germany
ISBN: 978-3-668-23779-7

This book at GRIN:

http://www.grin.com/en/e-book/324071/treatments-for-bpd-borderline-personality-disorder-an-annotated-bibliography

Danielle LaBeau

**Treatments for BPD (Borderline Personality Disorder).
An Annotated Bibliography**

GRIN Publishing

GRIN - Your knowledge has value

Since its foundation in 1998, GRIN has specialized in publishing academic texts by students, college teachers and other academics as e-book and printed book. The website www.grin.com is an ideal platform for presenting term papers, final papers, scientific essays, dissertations and specialist books.

Visit us on the internet:

http://www.grin.com/

http://www.facebook.com/grincom

http://www.twitter.com/grin_com

Treatments For Borderline Personality Disorder

Annotated Bibliography

Danielle Labeau

r). Dialectical Behavior Therapy (DBT) in the Treatment of Borderline Personality Disorder. *Journal of Psychiatric & Mental Health Nursing, 21*(6), 518–525. http://doi.org/10.1111/jpm.12116

This article begins with setting the stage that Dialectical Behavior Therapy (DBT) is a form of Cognitive Behavior Treatment (CBT) for borderline personality disorder (BPD). Borderline personality disorder is a compound psychological disorder that is shaped by the influence of dysregulation of emotion, behavior and cognition. Dialectics is the way in which someone with BPD might be able to understand changes with his or her contradictory views of these emotion, behavior, and cognition concretely. The purpose of understanding dialectics is to realize that there are two different opposing points of view at hand. DBT is a process of bringing these two points together and making the patient aware of these two opposing views and to fuse the two together.

DBT was first developed with the intention of looking at a person with BPD as an emotionally vulnerable person combined with a living environment that was not undermining those emotions (Harned, Banawan, & Lynch, 2006). Taking this into consideration, DBT uses multiple treatment tactics such as chain analysis, mindfulness, opposite action and validation, which all use emotional validation.

The therapist helps patients learn problem-solving skills in place of his or her unwanted behavior by using Chain analysis. Mindfulness is considered the key skill of DBT. Mindfulness is a skill that is taught to teach the person dealing with BPD to experience their emotions, thoughts, or what is going on in the environment around them in a non-judgmental way. Opposite action works in two different ways: behavioral exposure and cognitive modification. An example from another article to describe the behavioral exposure is to make the patient aware that when the emotion of anger is present and justified, the natural reaction is to attack. Instead, the skill taught to avoid the reaction to attack, is to avoid attacking mentally and physically. In place, the person might be able to use a new taught skill such as empathy (Harned, Banawan, & Lynch, 2006). Cognitive modification aids opposite action by changing the view of his or her emotional experience. Together behavioral exposure and cognitive modification comes together to change not only behaviors, but also the emotion associated with the behavior to create opposite action. Finally, one of the main keys for being a good therapist is validation of one's thoughts and feelings. When the therapist does this, the patient feels accepted and produces a positive and trusting environment for change.

The study in this article was to look at the five personality traits of those with BPD. The five personality traits are: neuroticism, extraversion, openness to experience, agreeableness and conscientiousness. Two groups of participants were chosen. The first group was on the waiting list to begin DBT or had just begun their 8-week skill-building module. The second group had already completed their DBT program within the past three years. The study was conducted by a questionnaire and was sent to all participants. The study showed that those who had not had DBT scored higher in neuroticism and lower consciousness than those who had undergone DBT. The conclusion is that further evidence is needed to determine the true effectiveness of DBT for those with BPD.

Davidson, K., Norrie, J., Tyrer, P., Gumley, A., Tata, P., Murray, H., & Palmer, S. (2006). The Effectiveness of Cognitive Behavior Therapy for Borderline Personality Disorder: Results From the Borderline Personality Disorder Study of Cognitive Therapy (boscot) Trial. *Journal of Personality Disorders, 20*(5), 450–465. http://doi.org/10.1521/pedi.2006.20.5.450

This article's hypothesis is that Cognitive Behavioral Therapy (CBT) can bring about quick and important changes in a patient suffering with Borderline Personality Disorder (BPD) in clinical settings. A randomized study was conducted between the dates of January 2002 through February 2005 at three United Kingdom locations. The patients were chosen based on eligibility, which was if they were between the ages of 18 and 65 years old and fit the criteria of BPD by showing at least 5 signs of BPD. The study was conducted using treatment as usual in addition to CBT.

Treatment as usual may have varied based on the therapist's abilities and each patient's needs and also included a wide variety of resources, including inpatient and outpatient programs, nurses and other qualified clinical services. CBT was used in addition in these patients to mature and change beliefs about themselves and others. Meanwhile, CBT was also used to help patients grow immature behavioral actions into behavior that would support social functioning.

The primary outcome was to determine if the suicidal acts, emergency related accidents, and psychiatric hospitalization was lessened. The secondary outcome was to determine if self-harm acts and acts not caused by accidents were lessened by combining CBT with treatment as usual. The primary outcome showed no significant differences using CBT and treatment as usual versus treatment as usual in regards to suicide attempt, hospitalization, or emergency related accidents. However, there was a significant reduction of suicidal acts due to CBT combined with treatment as usual, as opposed to just treatment as usual. The secondary outcome showed some significant differences with the addition of CBT in therapy.

Since that particular study, there have been others that do in fact prove that CBT in addition to treatment as usual has reduced suicidal behavior and levels of anxiety. CBT also may have brought about a change in beliefs but not a change in depression levels. It was determined by this article of study that further research might be conducted to explain under what conditions CBT might be most effective.

Jørgensen, C. R., Freund, C., Bøye, R., Jordet, H., Andersen, D., & Kjølbye, M. (2013). Outcome of Mentalization-Based and Supportive Psychotherapy in Patients with Borderline Personality Disorder: a Randomized Trial. *Acta Psychiatrica Scandinavica*, *127*(4), 305–317. http://doi.org/10.1111/j.1600-0447.2012.01923.x

This article started off by describing what BPD is. It is known to be one of the most difficult disorders to treat because of the complexity of psychosocial skills a person with BPD has. Often a person with BPD is very unstable in every aspect of life including relationships and work. This disorder is commonly found in women and is coupled with other personality disorders. Over time, however, no single treatment model has been used. The article does make mention that DBT was superior to all treatment as usual thus far.

The purpose of the study that was conducted tested two years worth of Mentalization based therapy (MBT) and two years of supportive group therapy in patients who were diagnosed with BPD. The study was conducted of 111 patients who were randomly assigned to either MBT or supportive group therapy. MBT consisted of 45 minute sessions weekly of therapy while supportive group therapy consisted of 1 ½ hour weekly sessions. Both groups of patients also participated in psycho-educational programs once a month for six months.

In this case, MBT was used to help separate the patient from the thoughts and feelings from the therapist and others and then to consider how his or her view might be different from those others. Mentalization is the ability to understand both behaviors, of the patient and others, and how they are connected with both mental states (Grohol & read, n.d.). Once that was established, the patients were taught interpersonal behaviors by working through series of events and emotions that had occurred in the patients' life. The supportive group focused on the individual of the group and supportive techniques were used by therapists and taught to members of the groups to help improve interpersonal behavior and reflect understanding.

The level of functioning was tested and self reported using the Revised Symptom Check List (SLC-90-R) questionnaire. Depression and anxiety were tested using the Beck Depression Inventory (BDI), and the Beck Anxiety Inventory (BAI). The Global Assessment of Functioning (GAF) was used to evaluate the severity of disturbance. The patients were asked to answer the questioners every three months. As a result, some patients refused to answer the questionnaires that resulted in a loss of data. The results showed that MBT was only greater to less intensive supportive group therapy on the GAF scale. All the other scales did show improvement in the patients as well. What can be said for sure is that both MBT and supportive group therapy are both effective in helping patients with BPD.

Nadort, M., Arntz, A., Smit, J. H., Giesen-Bloo, J., Eikelenboom, M., Spinhoven, P., … van Dyck, R. (2009). Implementation of Outpatient Schema Therapy for Borderline Personality Disorder: Study Design. *BMC Psychiatry*, *9*, 64. http://doi.org/http://dx.doi.org.hodges.idm.oclc.org/10.1186/1471-244X-9-64

This article begins with a brief description of what Schema Focused Therapy (SFT) is. SFT is a therapy that is derived from cognitive-behavioral therapy, attachment theory, and it uses Gestalt's techniques such as having the client confront emotional damages of the past. There were studies done in the recent past that showed that SFT reduced symptoms of suicides, fewer acts of self-harm, and an improvement in personality. BPD is considered changed when dysfunctional schemas are no longer controlling the person's life. Along with DBT and SFT it is believed that patients with BPD need extra support. For this purpose, the study in this article included a group that had crisis support after regular office hours and also had a group that did not have access to the extra crisis support.

Patients were able to join the randomized study with 60 patients with 30 therapists at several different locations in the Netherlands if they fit the DSM-IV criteria and were between the ages of 18-60. Patients were excluded if they suffer from one or more of other behavior disorders. Data for the study was collected once at the beginning of the study, three times in the middle of the study (6, 12, and 18 months) and then once three years after the study. Regular therapy sessions were conducted for 45 minutes twice every week for the first year and once every week for the following year.

The way change was recorded was by the ranges of behavioral, cognitive techniques that were shown in the therapist-client relationship, outside activities and relationships and recovery of past traumas. The conclusion of the study showed that the extra crisis therapy support was helpful, but not helpful enough to persuade therapists to want to be available after hours for what they would be paid.

Levy, K. N., Meehan, K. B., Kelly, K. M., Reynoso, J. S., Weber, M., Clarkin, J. F., & Kernberg, O. F. (2006). Change in Attachment Patterns and Reflective Function in a Randomized Control Trial of Tansference-Focused Psychotherapy for Borderline Personality Disorder. *Journal of Consulting and Clinical Psychology*, *74*(6), 1027–1040. http://doi.org/10.1037/0022-006X.74.6.1027

The beginning of this article addresses the depth of what BPD is. One of the things that researchers are noticing is that there is an attachment problem within the person suffering from BPD because they are unable to sustain relationships and because of this they feel loneliness, abandonment, and a lack of stability in themselves. This study will be the first of its kind to seek out possible changes in the attachment functions that a person with BPD has to deal with, as it appears attachment representations are a major underlying mechanism that most likely stemmed from childhood.

Attachment theory is categorized in five classifications: secure/autonomous (F), dismissing (D), enmeshed/preoccupied (E), unresolved/declassified (U/D), and cannot classify (CC). A secure/autonomous person is well organized and classifies his or her relationships as influential and valuable. Those who dismiss do not value relationships and even have a rough time recalling events from their past. Enmeshed/Preoccupied individuals often refer to their parents as being overbearing and guilt inducing. As adults these people will even continue to try to please parents out of passive aggressive behavior. These types of people also have a hard time putting sentences together to explain past and present relationships. Unresolved/disorganized is assigned to a person

8

when he or she cannot recall reasoning or the actual event of abuse or trauma. Cannot Classify is assigned to someone who shows a mixture of the other four classifications of attachment.

There were 90 participants who were between the ages of 18-50 who met the qualifications of BPD. The participants were either randomly assigned to TFP (transference focused psychotherapy), DBT (dialectical behavioral therapy), or SPT (supportive psychotherapy). TFP is a form of therapy that focuses on containing harmful acted out behaviors though clarification confrontation and identifying the interpersonal and relational patterns. The therapist focuses on helping by building the relationship between the clients and patient so they can apply insights they learn into other situations. DBT is a therapy that focuses on managing stress and accepting changing behaviors. SPT used by the therapist to provide comfort, advising, and listening to patient.

The assessment of attachment was deduced by the findings of the Adult Attachment Interview (AAI), which goes into depth about a person's past a current experiences and how these affected the adult. These results were also scored on the RF scare which ranges from -1 to 9 (barren mentalization to concrete reasoning). The results show that the RF, attachment awareness, and rates of being classified were increased. Although there was no change in resolution of loss or trauma, it was proven that TFP was more effective than the other two treatments.

Black, D. W., Allen, J., St. John, D., Pfohl, B., McCormick, B., & Blum, N. (2009). Predictors of Response to Systems Training for Emotional Predictability and Problem Solving (STEPPS) for Borderline Personality Disorder: An Exploratory Study. *Acta Psychiatrica Scandinavica, 120*(1), 53–61. http://doi.org/10.1111/j.1600-0447.2008.01340.x

This article provides a study that analyzes the STEPPS program as it related to people diagnosed with BPD. Subjects were selected for the study if they were 18 years old or older and fit the DSM-IV criteria. However, they could not be diagnosed with any other personality disorders, substance abuse issues, or have ever participated in a STEPPS program. The participants were randomly chosen to either do treatment as usual, or to do treatment as usual with the STEEPS program.

STEEPS is an out-patient treatment program for 20 weeks that manually treats patients with BPD. The first part of the program is to provide pychoeducation for BPD and bring awareness to the patient of his or her thoughts, feelings and actions. The program uses emotion and behavior management skills and additional cognitive behavioral skills. Finally, the program helps enforce goal setting, a healthy lifestyle, leisure, health monitoring, and avoiding self-harm.

The results of the study show that 15 STEPPS sessions may be the minimum for achieving the most improvement. The STEPPS plus treatment as usual participants who attended at least 15 sessions' improvement was much greater than the subjects who attended less that 15 STEPP sessions. There was some difficulty in maintaining the participants because they would drop out or not attend sessions as they were supposed to. Therefore, the results can be said to be limited.

Zanarini, M. C., & Frankenburg, F. R. (2003). Omega-3 fatty Acid Treatment of Women with Borderline Personality Disorder: A Double-Blind, Placebo-Controlled Pilot Study. *The American Journal of Psychiatry*, *160*(1), 167–9.

This article starts out with describing that medication for BPD is typically unhelpful.

However, there has been evidence and several other studies that have proved that Omega-3 fatty acids have improved other mood disorders, mainly among women. Omega-3 fatty acids include eicosapentaenoic acid and docosahexaenoic acid, which is most commonly found in seafood.

Twenty subjects were randomly assigned to either take a placebo or to take Omega-3 fatty acids for 8 weeks. These subjects were included if they met both the DIB-R and DSM-IV criteria. During the 8 weeks study, each subject was seen every week for the first month and every other week for the second month. Two scales, Modified Overt Aggression Scale and the Montgomery-Asberg Depression Rating Scale, were used and updated each week to show psychiatric ratings.

All members decided to stay in the study, thus making the results more accurate. Those who were treated with the Omega-3 fatty acid showed great reduction in their depression and aggression than those who took that placebo. The limitation of this study is that is was just done with women. The same study with men may have different outcomes.

References:

Harned, M. S., Banawan, S. F., & Lynch, T. R. (2006). Dialectical Behavior Therapy: An Emotion-Focused Treatment for Borderline Personality Disorder. *Journal of Contemporary Psychotherapy*, *36*(2), 67–75.

http://doi.org/http://dx.doi.org.hodges.idm.oclc.org/10.1007/s10879-006-9009-x

Grohol, J. M., & read, P. D. ~ 1 min. (n.d.). Mentalization Based Therapy (MBT). Retrieved March 4, 2016, from http://psychcentral.com/lib/mentalization-based-therapy-mbt/